FAMOUS SHIPWRECKS
GREAT LAKES SHIPWRECKS

by Michelle Parkin

Ideas for Parents and Teachers

Pogo Books let children practice reading informational text while introducing them to nonfiction features such as headings, labels, sidebars, maps, and diagrams, as well as a table of contents, glossary, and index.

Carefully leveled text with a strong photo match offers early fluent readers the support they need to succeed.

Before Reading

- "Walk" through the book and point out the various nonfiction features. Ask the student what purpose each feature serves.
- Look at the glossary together. Read and discuss the words.

Read the Book

- Have the child read the book independently.
- Invite him or her to list questions that arise from reading.

After Reading

- Discuss the child's questions. Talk about how he or she might find answers to those questions.
- Prompt the child to think more. Ask: Why do you think there are so many shipwrecks in the Great Lakes? Are you surprised large ships can sink in a lake?

Pogo Books are published by Jump!
5357 Penn Avenue South
Minneapolis, MN 55419
www.jumplibrary.com

Library of Congress Cataloging-in-Publication Data

Names: Parkin, Michelle, 1984- author.
Title: Great Lakes shipwrecks / by Michelle Parkin.
Description: Minneapolis, MN: Jump!, Inc., [2024]
Series: Famous shipwrecks | Includes index.
Audience: Ages 7-10
Identifiers: LCCN 2023034527 (print)
LCCN 2023034528 (ebook)
ISBN 9798889966623 (hardcover)
ISBN 9798889966630 (paperback)
ISBN 9798889966647 (ebook)
Subjects: LCSH: Shipwrecks—Great Lakes (North America) – Juvenile literature. | Great Lakes (North America) – History—Juvenile literature.
Classification: LCC G525 .P366 2024 (print)
LCC G525 (ebook)
DDC 910.4/520977–dc23/eng/20230807
LC record available at https://lccn.loc.gov/2023034527
LC ebook record available at https://lccn.loc.gov/2023034528

Editor: Alyssa Sorenson
Designer: Anna Peterson

Photo Credits: The Great Lakes Shipwreck Historical Society, cover; LINAYAYA LIN/Shutterstock, 1; aaron peterson.net/Alamy, 3; Anton Balazh/Shutterstock, 4; James.Pintar/Shutterstock, 5; Dominique Braud/Dembinsky Photo Associates/Alamy, 6; Photo12/Universal Images Group/Getty, 7; Jack Papes, Fairport Harbor, Ohio, 8-9; Thunder Bay National Marine Sanctuary/AP Images, 10-11; NOAA, 12-13, 20-21; Bob Campbell, 14-15; Danita Delimont/Alamy, 16-17; Michael Olson/iStock, 18; Iam_Anuphone/Shutterstock, 19; Lupe Ayala/Shutterstock, 23.

Printed in the United States of America at Corporate Graphics in North Mankato, Minnesota.

For Bob, Jasmine, and Avenue

TABLE OF CONTENTS

CHAPTER 1
Welcome to the Great Lakes 4

CHAPTER 2
Lost to the Lakes 6

CHAPTER 3
Sailing the Lakes Today 18

QUICK FACTS & TOOLS
Where They Sank in the Great Lakes 22
Glossary 23
Index 24
To Learn More 24

CHAPTER 1

· ·

WELCOME TO THE GREAT LAKES

Have you heard of the Great Lakes? There are five. They are Lake Superior, Lake Michigan, Lake Huron, Lake Erie, and Lake Ontario. They border the United States and Canada.

CANADA

LAKE SUPERIOR

LAKE HURON

LAKE ONTARIO

Great Lakes

LAKE ERIE

LAKE MICHIGAN

UNITED STATES

Ships sail the Great Lakes. Why? They **transport** goods such as coal and grain.

CHAPTER 2

· ·

LOST TO THE LAKES

The Great Lakes are larger than most. Sailing them can be dangerous. Storms and large waves **damage** ships. More than 6,000 have sunk in the Great Lakes.

On September 8, 1860, *Lady Elgin* was sailing on Lake Michigan. Hundreds of passengers were onboard. A storm came in. It was hard to see. Another boat hit and damaged *Lady Elgin*. Around 300 people died when the ship sank. The **shipwreck** was found in 1989.

Sultan

On September 24, 1864, *Sultan* was on Lake Erie. It was sailing through a storm. The ship's **hull** hit a **sandbar**. Water leaked in. Then waves flipped the ship over. It sank.

The shipwreck was found in the 1980s. Divers fully explored it in 2011. They took videos and photos of the wreck.

DID YOU KNOW?

Lake Erie is very **shallow**. Ships can scrape against rocks or sandbars.

One windy night in September 1894, *Ironton* was on Lake Huron. It hit another ship. It started sinking. Some of the **crew** jumped onto a **lifeboat**. But they couldn't get it off the ship in time. The lifeboat was pulled to the bottom of the lake with the *Ironton*.

People found the shipwreck in 2019. The lifeboat was still there, too.

Ironton

St. Peter

St. Peter was on Lake Ontario in October 1898. A snowstorm hit. Waves reached 20 feet (6.1 meters) high. Winds were very strong. *St. Peter* tipped to the side. Water flooded the ship. It sank to the bottom of the lake. The shipwreck was found in 1971.

TAKE A LOOK!

Why do ships sink in the Great Lakes? Take a look!

STORMS BRING STRONG WINDS

LARGE WAVES CAN DAMAGE OR TIP SHIPS

On November 10, 1975, the SS *Edmund Fitzgerald* sailed Lake Superior. It got caught in a storm. Waves reached 25 feet (7.6 m) high. No one knows for sure what happened to the ship. But experts believe it took on too much water. The ship sank beneath the waves. None of its crew survived.

In May 1976, *Edmund Fitzgerald* was found at the bottom of Lake Superior. Since then, many people have dived to see it.

In 1995, divers took a large bell from the ship. It is now in Michigan's Great Lakes Shipwreck Museum. You can see it!

WHAT DO YOU THINK?

The *Edmund Fitzgerald* sinking is a mystery. Think about what you know about shipwrecks. How do you think the *Edmund Fitzgerald* sank?

CHAPTER 3

· ·

SAILING THE LAKES TODAY

Many ships sail the Great Lakes. They carry goods to and from cities. People sail through the Great Lakes for fun. But the waters can still be dangerous.

Today, technology helps keep ships safe. Ships have good communication tools. People are better at tracking weather. With **GPS**, ships can see exactly where other boats are. This prevents **collisions**.

People search the Great Lakes for shipwrecks. They use **sonar** and **remotely operated vehicles (ROVs)** to study them. Divers sometimes go deep to look at the wrecks. We study shipwrecks to stay safe on the waters today.

WHAT DO YOU THINK?

Scientists study ships that have sunk in the Great Lakes. What do you think we can learn from these shipwrecks?

QUICK FACTS & TOOLS

WHERE THEY SANK IN THE GREAT LAKES

1. *Lady Elgin* was on Lake Michigan when she sank in 1860. Divers found the shipwreck in 1989.

2. *Sultan* sank in 1864 in Lake Erie. It was discovered in the 1980s.

3. In 1894, *Ironton* sank in Lake Huron. It wasn't found until 2019.

4. *St. Peter* sank during a snowstorm in 1898 in Lake Ontario. The shipwreck was discovered in 1971.

5. The SS *Edmund Fitzgerald* sank mysteriously in Lake Superior in 1975. The wreck was found the next year.

GLOSSARY

collisions: Sudden and violent strikings of two objects.

crew: A group of people who work on a ship.

damage: Harm.

GPS: Global Positioning System; a navigational tool that uses satellites to find something's exact location.

hull: The body of a ship.

lifeboat: A boat on a large ship that people use to get off the ship in emergencies.

remotely operated vehicles (ROVs): Unmanned underwater machines used to explore deep water.

sandbar: A ridge of sand in a lake.

shallow: Not deep.

shipwreck: The remains of a sunken ship.

sonar: A device or method used to find out how deep water is or where underwater objects are.

transport: To move from one place to another.

INDEX

crew 10, 15

divers 9, 16, 20

Edmund Fitzgerald 15, 16

GPS 19

Great Lakes Shipwreck Museum 16

Ironton 10

Lady Elgin 7

Lake Erie 4, 9

Lake Huron 4, 10

Lake Michigan 4, 7

Lake Ontario 4, 13

Lake Superior 4, 15, 16

lifeboat 10

remotely operated vehicles (ROVs) 20

sandbar 9

shallow 9

snowstorm 13

sonar 20

storms 6, 7, 9, 13, 14, 15

St. Peter 13

Sultan 9

transport 5

waves 6, 9, 13, 14, 15

wind 10, 13, 14

TO LEARN MORE

Finding more information is as easy as 1, 2, 3.

1. Go to www.factsurfer.com
2. Enter "GreatLakesshipwrecks" into the search box.
3. Choose your book to see a list of websites.

FACT SURFER